Stand Up, Friend, With Me

STAND UP, FRIEND, WITH ME

by

Edward Field

GROVE PRESS, INC. / NEW YORK

Library of Congress Catalog Card Number: 63–12839

First Evergreen Edition 1964

ACKNOWLEDGMENTS—A number of these poems were previously pub-
lished in the following books and periodicals: *A New Folder, Beloit
Poetry Journal, Botteghe Oscure, Evergreen Review, New Directions
in Prose and Poetry* (New Directions, vol. 13, 1951; vol. 16, 1957),
*Paris Review, Partisan Review, Poetry, Prairie Schooner, The New
American Poetry: 1945–1960* (Grove Press, 1960).

Manufactured in the United States of America

The Lamont Poetry Selection for 1962

(A first publication award sponsored by
The Academy of American Poets)

To my Mother and Father

CONTENTS

PART I

GREECE

Hydra

This island whose name means water
Never had gods and temples as other Greek islands had;
It never was the home of monsters with ferocious heads
And maybe it wasn't even there.

But a few centuries ago
As though it had just risen from the sea
Men saw stones and pine trees on the slopes
And with the stones made houses and with the trees made ships.

And as naturally as fish swim
The ships went sailing;
And as naturally as the sun rises
The boys grew into heroes and sailed to war.

But the heroes were foolhardy as heroes are
So although they were brave and did amazing things
The ships were sunk at last
And the handsome heroes lay on the ocean floor.

Wars over, fame won, the island settled down,
But with the trees all gone the soil blew away to sea;
The houses began to crumble,
And the island bleached in the sun to anonymity.

The name means water but now even the wells are drying
And no one expects the rock to grow trees again;
While the waters push gently on its shores
Waiting for the island to sink quietly back in the sea.

Donkeys

They are not silent like workhorses
Who are happy or indifferent about the plow and wagon;
Donkeys don't submit like that
For they are sensitive
And cry continually under their burdens;
Yes, they are animals of sensibility
Even if they aren't intelligent enough
To count money or discuss religion.

Laugh if you will when they heehaw
But know that they are crying
When they make that noise that sounds like something
Between a squawking water pump and a foghorn.

And when I hear them sobbing
I suddenly notice their sweet eyes and ridiculous ears
And their naive bodies that look as though they never grew up
But stayed children, as in fact they are;
And being misunderstood as children are
They are forced to walk up mountains
With men and bundles on their backs.

Somehow I am glad that they do not submit without a protest
But as their masters are of the deafest
The wails are never heard.

I am sure that donkeys know what life should be
But, alas, they do not own their bodies;
And if they had their own way, I am sure
That they would sit in a field of flowers
Kissing each other, and maybe
They would even invite us to join them.

For they never let us forget that they know
(As everyone knows who stays as sweet as children)
That there is a far better way to spend time;
You can be sure of that when they stop in their tracks
And honk and honk and honk.

And if I tried to explain to them
Why work is not only necessary but good,
I am afraid that they would never understand
And kick me with their back legs
As commentary on my wisdom.

So they remain unhappy and sob
And their masters who are equally convinced of being right
Beat them and hear nothing.

Goats

Our insides are not awfully different:
Like a tight sweater the skin pulls over the head;
A slit, and the entrails bulge,
Quite clean! I had imagined them bloody.
And how familiar their appearance:
Sausages never disgusted us before
So why should they now in the raw?

Not at all imagining themselves in the nibbled-at position,
A chicken pecks cozily at lean
And a cat chews a piece of fat.

Of course, by now there is no resemblance anymore
To a goat; more like a meat market:
The behind has turned into steaks
And all the other parts now have culinary names.
The gross butcher with small eyes and a stupid forehead
Starts hosing away the pools of blood,
And the expression on his face slowly changes
From Eternal Destroyer to haggling merchant.

Now the buyers in procession march
Joyfully to market
As they never do when relatives die,
For they know it would be ridiculous,
Even though unskinned he looks like us,
To mourn a goat.

And besides there is nothing to mourn;
Certainly not his death
While he cooks in peace in various kitchens,
Nor his life when he leapt from rock to rock.

And then he ba-a-a-d and died:
So let us be as joyful as he was,
Eating our goat stew,
Making the movement of dancing and the noise of singing,
Taking each others' bodies in our arms
And then filing simply off to bed.

Greece

This is a country where miracles occur:
The probability is in the air
That statues turn human if you kiss them;
And at any moment one expects a god
To step from the marble column, and indeed
They could not have remained standing for so long
If they were not still inhabited by gods.

Naturally one doesn't always expect to see
People wearing snakes for hair
Or satyrs chasing youths
Or charming gods turning into still more charming bulls,
But such things do occur.
One knows, for example, that men and goats
Copulate with fertile success.
Look now at this goat walking up the road
Led by a young Greek with a definite goatish look:
Goats and Greeks have lived together for so long
That there are many similarities,
Especially when they sing.

And of course if the Greek is not a shepherd
He is a seaman; for the sea is everywhere
And still sailed by sleek ships
And the monsters that habitually swallow them;
And everywhere are islands where sailors grow
Wise like olives to the lore of salt.

Though not quite as much admitted openly nowadays
The favorite occupation still is sex
And it is easy to know why
When you see their bodies as beautiful as ever,

With one exception, the Greeks that go to America.
Of course they come back to Greece if they can as we all do,
But they return with something gone out of them:
I suppose they sacrifice their gods to a foreign one
And lose their own divinity.

Anyway, I'd have known the Greeks anywhere
Even though I'd forgotten details like diarrhea
And the Sea Urchins that tempt the tender foot.
And it's good to be back after two thousand years
To find that Greece is still the country
Where the sea and the olive and the goat
Speak with personal voices to a race of men.

Icarus

Only the feathers floating around the hat
Showed that anything more spectacular had occurred
Than the usual drowning. The police preferred to ignore
The confusing aspects of the case,
And the witnesses ran off to a gang war.
So the report filed and forgotten in the archives read simply
"Drowned," but it was wrong: Icarus
Had swum away, coming at last to the city
Where he rented a house and tended the garden.

"That nice Mr. Hicks" the neighbors called him,
Never dreaming that the gray, respectable suit
Concealed arms that had controlled huge wings
Nor that those sad, defeated eyes had once
Compelled the sun. And had he told them
They would have answered with a shocked, uncomprehending
  stare.
No, he could not disturb their neat front yards;
Yet all his books insisted that this was a horrible mistake:
What was he doing aging in a suburb?
Can the genius of the hero fall
To the middling stature of the merely talented?

And nightly Icarus probes his wound
And daily in his workshop, curtains carefully drawn,
Constructs small wings and tries to fly
To the lighting fixture on the ceiling:
Fails every time and hates himself for trying.

He had thought himself a hero, had acted heroically,
And dreamt of his fall, the tragic fall of the hero;
But now rides commuter trains,
Serves on various committees,
And wishes he had drowned.

Ruth and Naomi

If one is a Jew who has a history
—Meaning simply to remember and be sad—
Then Ruth became a Jewess
When Naomi's kisses in her gentile blood
Turned the rumors garrulous in her veins.

How easy for men! They offer up their foreskins.
How strange she felt before this god
Who was, after all, only a voice in the clouds!
So she solved the question as later other gentiles did:
She made the one she loved her godhead.

At first the rabbis were shocked at this liaison,
But what could be done? She ate no pork
And obeyed all the sacred laws;
So, being wise, they turned it into a moral lesson
And loved her, since she was lovable.

And when the people learned the official approval
All of Israel blessed this union
(Which they had been secretly admiring anyway)
As Ruth and Naomi, lip to vaginal lip,
Proclaimed their love throughout the land.

Song

as the musician embraces
the body of his guitar
as the man caresses
the unawakened girl

over this paper I
put hands to my desire
that your waking eyes may see
your thighs respond and open
warm mouth and a thousand arms
reach beloved poem for me

Aladdin

Only Aladdin could tell, of all the lamps at the flea market,
Which one was magical, and even he
Didn't know a thing about its magic.
He chose the one disguised as a teapot,
Paying the usual price, a penny, to the dealer;
And the moment he had it in his hands he knew
What until then he had no idea of:
How to make it work.

With his house key he scratched away the cruddy surface:
Pure gold beneath, confirming what he had suspected;
And when he polished it up,
From the spout there rose a dragon breathing fire,
And 'thouten a blink of eye he seized it by the tail
Swinging it wide with all his might and main
And lo! it changed to a genie fore his very eyes
Who knelt and said, "My master."

There by the cemetery is the market
Where the junkmen spread their wares,
All the things we use, grow sick of, and throw away.
Go there, friend: For he who dares to pick the magic lamp
From row on row identically tarnished,
Knowing a dragon will issue from its wick,
And swing the monster by his jaggedy tail
Will have the power of a giant at his bidding.

Prologue

Look, friend, at this universe
With its spiral clusters of stars
Flying out all over space
Like bedsprings suddenly busting free;
And in this galaxy, the sun
Fissioning itself away,
Surrounded by planets, prominent in their dignity,
And bits and pieces running wild;
And this middling planet
With a lone moon circling round it.

Look, friend, through the fog of gases at this world
With its skin of earth and rock, water and ice,
With various creatures and rooted things;
And up from the bulging waistline
To this land of concrete towers,
Its roads swarming like a hive cut open,
Offshore to this island, long and fishshaped,
Its mouth to a metropolis,
And in its belly, this village,
A gathering of families at a crossways,
And in this house, upstairs and through the wide open door
Of the front bedroom with a window on the world,
Look, friend, at me.

PART II

A VIEW OF JERSEY

In the Morning

Often in the morning the fog is thick over Jersey,
Sometimes, like today, lifting later on
To reveal with the clarity of a dream
The wide river with its traffic, the cluttered far shore,
And the hills beyond where hidden towns
Send up spires like messages.

The river is never terribly obscured
Even when the land beyond is absolutely white,
And I can see the ferry leave the shore
With a load of commuters like refugees from a land
Where faces have no face, and bodies only exist
If you put your arms around them.

They come to the city where I am
Although they do not find me
Nor even know that they are searching for me;
And as the morning progresses with its growing clarity
There *is* a world over there after all,
Anyway, for a while, precise as a dream, perfect and grimy,
Until another night and its temperatures
Pulls down the fog from the air and obliterates it.

A Bill to My Father

I am typing up bills for a firm to be sent to their clients.
It occurs to me that firms are sending bills to my father
Who has that way an identity I do not often realize.
He is a person who buys, owes, and pays,
Not papa like he is to me.
His creditors reproach him for not paying on time
With a bill marked "Please Remit."
I reproach him for never having shown his love for me
But only his disapproval.
He has a debt to me too
Although I have long since ceased asking him to come across;
He does not know how and so I do without it.
But in this impersonal world of business
He can be communicated with:
With absolute assurance of being paid
The boss writes "Send me my money"
And my father sends it.

Notes from a Slave Ship

It is necessary to wait until the boss's eyes are on you
Then simply put your work aside,
Slip a fresh piece of paper in the typewriter,
And start to write a poem.

Let their eyes boggle at your impudence;
The time for a poem is the moment of assertion,
The moment when you say I exist—
Nobody can buy my time absolutely.

Nobody can buy me even if I say, Yes I sell.
There I am sailing down the river,
Quite happy about the view of the passing towns,
When I find that I have jumped overboard.

There is always a long swim to freedom.
The worst of it is the terrible exhaustion
Alone in the water in the darkness,
The shore a fading memory and the direction lost.

The Ocean Liner

Seen against the landscape of New Jersey
The liners going upriver are enormous
Rocking in their wake the ferryboats
That cross from shore to shore.

                              I prefer the ferries.
What have I to do with ocean monsters?
The liners look good at sea where they belong
And the USE MOORE PAINT sign on the waterfront.

I don't want Moses to walk on earth again
And lead us, even to the promised land
If there is one anywhere. I accept
The size of man, the scope of his work, and his failure.

If someone is to lead us let it be
A small man who doesn't ask us to follow
But just goes for his own heart's sake; someone
Who talks a little silly sometimes.

                              Well,
Talking of leaders, ignoring them is better
Till they go away; and if they won't,
Survival, hard now, might get a little harder.
Maybe I will think about it next year.

Meanwhile evening has fallen, the USE MOORE PAINT sign
Is flashing its useless message, the great ship
Has gone, and I can look at the view again
That I so depend on to free me from this office
For trips to Hoboken and back like the ferryboat makes:
The perfect space to read my heart in.

My Coldwater Flat

Now that it is winter my coldwater flat is cold:
The morning alarm wakes my seedy eyes to their first heroic
      look;
If they shut just once all is lost.
I light the oven that barely pushes out a bell of warmth,
Shave a ragged face that I do not dare study,
And brush the traces of digestion out of my mouth.
Saliva flows, my arms
Struggle with the clothes like with an enemy.
The toilet is far beyond this small place of comfort,
And it is only at the extremest necessity
That I dare to bare my behind:
Truly I am man braving the elements.

And only now, blinking behind my typewriter
In the dry warmth commerce provides its dependents
Can I appreciate the miracle that got me out of bed
And made me leave behind my strange and lovely dreams
For the world and its miseries, mankind and his hungers,
For a life of goose pimples and sweat
And the rare overwhelming flush of love.

Union City

Union City this morning is all shell pink and mist blue,
A place that doesn't exist except from here.
If you go there they have signs up "POETS KEEP OUT"
And with good reason, for you know what poets do
To dark alleys like those where rats are the guardians
Who can be led by the slightly mad.
Alcoholics and trigger men are there to insure
That the virgin and the whore are each in her proper room
Never to meet unless an earthquake shakes down a smokestack.

If from here Union City is a city of dreams,
From there New York is an island paradise;
The Hudson might be the Pacific itself.
And even though there are identical slums here,
You can walk out of them leaving behind the derelicts
Lying in their urine in doorways
To places where the winds of the world
Bring news of adventurers.

Even if you escape the seven pitfalls Union City presents
And walk out of it into the nation pink and blue in the morning
        mist,
You only find that it vanishes as you approach it
And you stranded among bitter mouths
That wear smiles like billboards.

From there on luck takes over
And it's anybody's guess as to what will become of you.
From there on you have to trust to your heart
Which often needs more than one lifetime to make a man.
But it's the only navigator you have
With a chance to get you somewhere where you want to go,
Through serpent-ruled swamps, magical forests,
Ghost-ridden infernos, into the open world
Where children and rabbits play among the sumac.

The Dirty Floor

The floor is dirty:
Not only the soot from the city air
But a surprising amount of hair litters the room.
It is hard to keep up with. Even before
The room is all swept up it is dirty again.

We are shedding more than we realize.
The amount of hair I've shed so far
Could make sixty of those great rugs
The Duke of China killed his weavers for,
And strangle half the sons of Islam.

Time doesn't stop even while I scrub the floor
Though it seems that the mind empties like a bathtub,
That all the minds of the world go down the drain
Into the sewer; but hair keeps falling
And not for a moment can the floor be totally clean.

What is left of us after years of shitting and shedding?
Are we whom our mothers bore or some stranger now
With the name of son, but nameless,
Continually relearning the same words
That mean, with each retelling, less.

He whom you knew is a trail of leavings round the world.
Renewal is a lie: Who I was has no more kisses.
Barbara's fierce eyes were long ago swept up from her floor.
A stranger goes by the name of Marianne; it is not she,
Nor for that matter was the Marianne I knew.

The floor having accumulated particles of myself
I call it dirty; dirty, the streets thick with the dead;
Dirty, the thick air I am used to breathing.
I am alive at least. Quick, who said that?
Give me the broom. The leftovers sweep the leavings away.

Spring

The new warmth of spring has raised a mist
Obscuring the vista that through the winter
Made this office a platform for speculation
And me a quite tranquil anchorite.

Now, itchy in my tweed pants
I'm ready to leave the city and go,
But I would have to go like a blind man
(For what difference if the eye dies or the sun?)
And stumble over rocks and fences.

Present me with a crossroads clear,
That's easy; but today there's a full
Three-hundred-and-sixty degrees of possibility,
Like the fledgling in the nest has
Before he leaps out into space.

A sparrow flies from window ledge to ground;
A plane buzzes off westward;
A ship moves down the river to the sea;
The street says One-Way and the auto follows:
Each has a course to travel and a place to rest.
When I look for a sign there is none.

If I were naked I think my body
Would know where to go of its own accord;
In the spring mist compounded with soot, barefoot,
By the breeze on my skin and the feel of the stones
I would go, not in a straight line of course,
But this way and that, as human nature goes,
Finding, if not the place, the way there.

The Telephone

My happiness depends on an electric appliance
And I do not mind giving it so much credit
With life in this city being what it is
Each person separated from friends
By a tangle of subways and buses
Yes my telephone is my joy
It tells me that I am in the world and wanted
It rings and I am alerted to love or gossip
I go comb my hair which begins to sparkle
Without it I was like a bear in a cave
Drowsing through a shadowy winter
It rings and spring has come
I stretch and amble out into the sunshine
Hungry again as I pick up the receiver
For the human voice and the good news of friends

Sonny Hugg Rides Again

I'm divorcing the view of Jersey
For a view of Manhattan.
Over in Brooklyn there is a window
That I mean to sit before.
My devotion shall be absolute
Like my faithfulness as a child
To Little Orphan Annie, Tom Mix,
And after dinner The Lone Ranger.

Here everything is plain to see,
The river and the Jersey landscape;
But over in Brooklyn there are dolphins under the bridge
Hawks over it and sailors do hornpipes by the shore.
Balloons ascend with poets flinging leaflets to the cheering
      crowds;
A carousel on a swan boat cruises the glassy waters
Playing French waltzes and Wagner.
Here, there are smoke, strikes, and hot-dog stands;
There, lovers swimming bare-ass off the piers.

The heart does a flip-flop and Sonny Hugg goes east a mile
Facing the same direction but with a new view of it,
The complete island for a vision not the desolate nation.
It is the holiest of mysteries:
He is walking around and not a soul can tell
What adventures are rocking his heart
And where his legs are taking him.

What Grandma Knew

The office feels like a sealed glass case today.
The air conditioning dates from the thirties.
That means it is ten years younger than I am.
Neither of us is working too well.

Outside the summer is going on for the outside world
But time is dragging me unwillingly into winter.
I ask myself my favorite question
"Why must I work for a living?"

This has no answer besides being irrelevant.
Old Italian men are fond of saying "No work, no eat."
And I guess that sums things up,
It says the world is so, and just accept it.

If you're famous, life is fun;
If you're not, you live like others do,
And go to the same death of the heart
Long before the hairs finally all fall out of your head.

If I had banjo eyes I'd strum a tune:
"My grandma always said, Alone is a stone.
But by the time life got through with grandma
She was glad to be alone."

Who Is Sylvia?

Who is Sylvia?
She whom I met last Saturday night,
The party and the hangover.
What is she?
Full of strange energy
Like the pear I ate with the pink cheek.
Who am I when I am with you, Sylvia?
In the mirror of your laughter
I hardly recognize myself.
I see myself as I really am, handsome, brave, and true.
Skepticism shrinks me,
But you set me growing like a field of daisies:
You lie down in me and role around: it tickles.
Who is Sylvia?
She gives me the courage to ask.
I step out of my clothes when I think of her.
Christmas balls drop from the tree into the snow
With a sizzle.

Is she Edwige Feuillere?
Yes she is.
Beautiful women are never so lucky
As when a poet appreciates them:
He creates her and she saves the life
That he is always about to throw away.
She takes his hand and they go off
Into the difficult valley of desire.

Who is Sylvia?
She is my mission.
I fly to where she keeps her legendary cities of the jungle:
Bathe my feet, priest, robe me in red
And lead me to the river where the black mud of centuries flows:
We are carried off to sea to build a new continent.

Three horns announce midnight and the world is awash:
Who is Sylvia?
Sylvia, Sylvia, Sylviana,
She is the wave.

Poem for the Left Hand

Cancer strikes and I lose my left hand:
My whole life has to be reorganized
Since I can no longer earn my living as a typist.
I am now one of the obviously crippled
Although to tell the truth
I have been one of them for as long as I can remember,
And all those years I was aware
That I was in the state of cancer if not cancerous yet.
My concern was laughed at.

Life is simpler now; no one will dream
Of looking further than my handless arm
For my deformity; it will be a hook to hang my troubles on,
For of course I shall wear a hook in its place
Rather than one of those prosthetic appliances,
And I shall join the ranks of other men
Who blame their troubles on similar unalterable situations
Such as the wife, or automation (the machine replacing the hand),
And they are right. Something is wrong with people
Who say it's me that's wrong, my nature needs changing.
Our nature is god's various will
And each oddity precious for the evolving animal kingdom.

Now that I am back to hunt and peck
I thank God for granting me this reprieve
From that endless unraveling of my nature.
Knots are too difficult for one hand to be bothered with:
Now I cut them through and laugh for the liberation.

The Statue of Liberty

All the ships are sailing away without me.
Day after day I hear their horns announcing
To the wage earners at their desks
That it is too late to get aboard.

They steam out of the harbor
With the statue of a French woman waving them good-by
Who used to be excellent to welcome people with
But is better lately for departures.

The French gave her to us as a reminder
Of their slogan and our creed
Which hasn't done much good
Because we have turned a perfectly good wilderness
Into a place nice to visit but not to live in.

Forever a prisoner in the harbor
On her star-shaped island of gray stones
She has turned moldy looking and shapeless
And her bronze drapery stands oddly into the wind.

From this prison-like island
I watch the ships sailing away without me
Disappearing one by one, day after day,
Into the unamerican distance,

And in my belly is one sentence: *Set Freedom Free*,
As the years fasten me into place and attitude,
Hand upraised and face into the wind
That no longer brings tears to my eyes.

PART III

GRAFFITI

A Journey

When he got up that morning everything was different:
He enjoyed the bright spring day
But he did not realize it exactly, he just enjoyed it.

And walking down the street to the railroad station
Past magnolia trees with dying flowers like old socks
It was a long time since he had breathed so simply.

Tears filled his eyes and it felt good
But he held them back
Because men didn't walk around crying in that town.

And waiting on the platform at the station
The fear came over him of something terrible about to happen:
The train was late and he recited the alphabet to keep hold.

And in its time it came screeching in
And as it went on making its usual stops,
People coming and going, telephone poles passing,

He hid his head behind a newspaper
No longer able to hold back the sobs, and willed his eyes
To follow the rational weavings of the seat fabric.

He didn't do anything violent as he had imagined.
He cried for a long time, but when he finally quieted down
A place in him that had been closed like a fist was open,

And at the end of the ride he stood up and got off that train:
And through the streets and in all the places he lived in later on
He walked, himself at last, a man among men,
With such radiance that everyone looked up and wondered.

Sonny Hugg and the Porcupine

This baby porcupine squeezing into a crevice of rock
Could be hauled out into the open,
Poked with a stick, and otherwise toyed with,
But cute as he was he couldn't be kissed.

Love rose tender in the heart of Sonny Hugg
And he dreamed impossible dreams.
But all those bristles! His mind twisted and turned
To find a workable solution.

To hug this improbable child was important to him,
The child willing or no, and who could say it wasn't willing.
Maybe the Gillette, the garden shears . . . No, without those spurs
This creature would be unlovable as a rat.

Sonny was versatile but this defeated him.
He faced reality. A porcupine for a lover?
Alas, he would have to settle for those creations
Not quite as darling but with bodies good for hugging.

An Event

Before the blond horsemen rode into our village
We held a hasty council to decide how to greet them.
It was planned that we would hide the women in the woods,
Cover our weapons with our sleeping mats in the huts
And greeting them politely
Neither encourage them to stay nor leave.

But when the hoofs raised a sudden dust in the square
Our hearts were beating so wildly
That nothing happened as we had planned it.
We came out all smiles throwing our weapons at their feet
And we feasted them, offering them our gods
And brought them our women
Whom they accepted with thin curved smiles.
And in the morning they drew a map of the area,
Counted the inhabitants and livestock,
And rode away with our silver ornaments.

Life went on as before and yet
Did we imagine it or were there fewer births than before?
The corn grew smaller
And not that things had been prosperous
(Our living had always been a scratching in the dust)
But year by year things seemed to diminish.
Now the young men go off to work in the factories
Putting on tight outlandish trousers and cutting their hair.
Even the women leave: They slip off at night
And return to visit later, slim and strangely garbed,
Talking without opening their mouths wide.

Perhaps now this is only a place to come home to,
To repeat the stories that everyone knows by heart,
And to look at the dusty flowers
And the children who will be going away soon
Playing naked and dirty among the chickens.

Trees

Here is the truth about trees:
I would no more be familiar with them than with a tiger.
Not that they will bite,
(They will only eat you up when you are dead, and your dog)
But they are of the same order of wildness.
I look at them carelessly only through the window
As the beasts in the zoo;
Even then I smell their odor named "Beware."

And walking by them down the road
I have to grant their right to possession of the earth
For they grow in perfect obedience to the laws of nature:
On this ball rolling through the heavens
Their million sucking roots take grip like claws,
Trunks rise and open into fierce branches and glittering leaves,
And they stand up in the sky,
Heads waving among the stars,
Risking outer space with its terrifying view:
The giant breed, of which we are the pigmies.

Graffiti

Blessings on all the kids who improve the signs in the subways:
They put a beard on the fashionable lady selling soap,
Fix up her flat chest with the boobies of a chorus girl,
And though her hips be wrapped like a mummy
They draw a hairy cunt where she should have one.

The bathing beauty who looks pleased
With the enormous prick in her mouth, declares
"Eat hair pie; it's better than cornflakes."
And the little boy in the tarzan suit eating white bread
Now has a fine pair of balls to crow about.

And as often as you wash the walls and put up your posters,
When you go back to the caged booth to deal out change
The bright-eyed kids will come with grubby hands.
Even if you watch, you cannot watch them all the time,
And while you are dreaming, if you have dreams anymore,

A boy and girl are giggling behind an iron pillar;
And although the train pulls in and takes them on their way
Into a winter that will freeze them forever,
They leave behind a wall scrawled all over with flowers
That shoot great drops of gism through the sky.

Song

I wish this paper were a stage
    and I an actor

then I'd walk simply to the footlights
    and sing of freedom
raging in the blood like wine

and kneeling before my lady
    speak my love
and all men's hearts would beat with mine

The Charmed Pool

At the charmed pool swarming with lower forms of life,
The flying, the crawling, the swimming, and the stationary,
Prince Charming looked around and wondered
Which of these creatures was the Princess
Who, the story said, was victim of a witch's curse
And waited for his kiss to reappear.

He was willing to try this kissing game
Even if a snake or a stone wasn't his idea of a good time.
To begin he chose a green frog with a gummy eye
And waded after it into the water feeling ridiculous
But with a sense of fulfilling prophecy.
Oh prince, prince, will you never grow up?

He caught the amphibian in his hand
And planted a kiss where he guessed its mouth was
And Prince Foolish, still pimpled from self-abuse,
Swooning with the same old admiration,
Was in his arms. He dropped him flat.
This magic can be an odd occupation.

He set about kissing all the creatures
Like the game of knock-knock-who's-there:
A dragonfly turned into Jack the Jew-Killer,
A mushroom into Miss Venom of the grammar school,
And soon there were lots of unpleasant people sitting around.
That witch had excellent taste in whom to banish.

Finally from a stone he got a princess,
Not his Princess to be sure, but the orphan princess,
With a calculated tear running down her nose
And crossed eyes that said, "Pity me."
He had; until he found her in the scullery with his uncle,
Praying at the head and sinning at the tail.

This had gone far enough; the Princess obviously wasn't there.
He took off his Prince costume
Revealing a quite attractive but ordinary young man
Who no longer knew what to do or where to go.
According to the story he found his princess at last
But, reader, do you really think he did?

This charming Prince who thought life had a happy ending,
I don't like to leave him like that naked by the pool,
The legend on the ground like a heap of worn-out clothing.
But if I said anything definite it would just be made up.
When a man tries the charmed pool and fails
What can he do if he doesn't die of it?

Is he wandering about the forest waiting to be found?
By whom? For what? He'll be a heap of bones by then.
Did he find the road back to where he came from?
And learn like us to live from day to day
Eating what's to eat and making love with what's available?
And did he ever fall in love again?

Unwanted

The poster with my picture on it
Is hanging on the bulletin board in the Post Office.

I stand by it hoping to be recognized
Posing first full face and then profile

But everybody passes by and I have to admit
The photograph was taken some years ago.

I was unwanted then and I'm unwanted now
Ah guess ah'll go up echo mountain and crah.

I wish someone would find my fingerprints somewhere
Maybe on a corpse and say, You're it.

Description: Male, or reasonably so
White, but not lily-white and usually deep-red

Thirty-fivish, and looks it lately
Five-feet-nine and one-hundred-thirty pounds: no physique

Black hair going gray, hairline receding fast
What used to be curly, now fuzzy

Brown eyes starey under beetling brow
Mole on chin, probably will become a wen

It is perfectly obvious that he was not popular at school
No good at baseball, and wet his bed.

His aliases tell his history: Dumbell, Good-for-nothing,
Jewboy, Fieldinsky, Skinny, Fierce Face, Greaseball, Sissy.

Warning: This man is not dangerous, answers to any name
Responds to love, don't call him or he will come.

The Half-Wit

A half-witted boy used to hang around Georgie's shop
(Retarded, they call it nowadays). Other people
Teased him, punished him, or chased him,
But Georgie just let him alone and listened,
While he sharpened saws and fixed flat tires,
To whatever he had to say which wasn't usually much.

One day the boy came out with this remark
(Georgie remembered it afterwards), "You know, Georgie?
I've just learned that boys are different from girls."
And how he learned that I don't know
Because he hadn't been molesting anyone,
But he figured it out somehow, or perhaps
He grew into the knowledge by some process of ripening.
Anyway, he had a fit that evening
As though the knowledge were causing in him
Some violent readjustment that he couldn't bear.

They called him retarded, but just as he was catching up
They got scared and put him away in a public institution.
That was a pretty important discovery he made
And one that I've been long in finding out myself.
It's not only half-wits that are ignorant,
Nor does whole-wit make the learning easier.

Nausea

It wasn't just the drink but the drink helped:
Suddenly he was aware he had been nauseous all his life
And all the food he hadn't wanted yet had eaten
Brought him now to the point of gagging.

A good puke was what he needed, a month of puking out
A lifetime of indigestibles,
But there was a terrible stricture in his chest
And he could hardly breathe properly, much less vomit.

He remembered when he still threw up
Onto the eating tray of his highchair
And the years afterwards when he kept it down:
Yet in spite of food, he wasted away.

You're skinny, the world accused.
I'm full up, he answered and went to his room
And read books and dreamed of exorbitant fame.
Sometimes he tried to cry but it never worked.

He gradually stopped feeling anything but humiliation
And when he tried to imagine punching a bully in the nose
Which in his circumstances would have been justified
His arm, as if paralyzed, couldn't move.

He survived school somehow and the army
By obedience, humility, and a desire to please.
And by not farting among the literary
He even passed for a sophisticate.

It need not be said that he shit rarely and then in dry lumps:
Even before the sergeant refused permission when cramps came
The teacher had a rule that you raise your hand
And ask to go: He learned to hold it in.

Needless to say he became impotent quite young
And even reconciled himself to that.
He didn't cross his eyes and turn to stone
But went on living somehow.

Do you think he was an unpleasant person? A dull one?
He wasn't. People liked him
And even thought him something special,
Praising his vivid complexion and his sparkling eyes.

Do you think he liked the thing he had become?
He didn't. And until this very night,
He hadn't felt such a desire to puke, or burst.
Excuse, reader, the stain on the whiteness of this page.

The Snowfish

As oceans are to porpoises
The snowdrift to the snowfish is.
The snowfish swims down with the snow
And tunnels in the drifts below.

Some creatures move in air or mud,
Moles in earth and worms in wood,
Owls in hollow trunks of trees:
Many the shapes of nature's fancies.

His various fishy cousins swim
In water for a medium.
These he resembles more or less
In iridescent nakedness.

Little about him can be taught
By scientific schools of thought.
He does not seem to fit the rules
That work for those who swim in schools.

And though great numbers of him fall
The snowfish won't conform at all.
The photograph you try to take
Will melt him quicker than a snowflake.

You cannot catch him with a line:
When thickets of snow are coming down
You know the snowfish is around
By the knocking on your windowblind,

But that's the only sound he makes—
Music makes him dance a bit;
Most of all he loves good wit,
But he's never taken any bait.

All we can say of him is this:
He must be accepted as he is;
You must allow him to exist:
He might be something you have missed.

To each a season when he sleeps;
To each a weather when he goes.
Today's the day when wise men see
The snowfish frisking in the snow.

PART IV

A NEW CYCLE

A New Cycle

My father buying me the bicycle that time
Was an unusual thing for him to do.
He believed that a parent's duty meant the necessities:
Food, clothing, shelter, and music lessons.

I had hardly dared to ask him for the bike
And I didn't believe he really meant to buy me one
Until I saw him take out the money and hand it over—
Eight dollars secondhand, but newly painted, and good rubber.

And I couldn't thank him, a hug was out of the question with us,
So I just got up on it and rode a ways shakily
And then I made him ride it—
He didn't even know he was supposed to say it was a good bike.

I rode off on it into a new life, paper route, pocket money,
Dances in other towns where the girls found me attractive,
And sexual adventures that would have made my father's hair
Stand up in horror had he known.

Daddy I can thank you now for the bike you gave me
Which meant more to me than you knew, or could have stood to
        know.
I rode away to everywhere it could take me, until finally
It took me to this nowhere, this noplace I am now.

I just passed my thirty-fifth birthday,
The end of a seven-year cycle and the beginning of a new one,
And sure enough I woke up the first day quite empty,
Everything over, with nothing to do and no ideas for the future.

Daddy whom I now can hug and kiss
Who gives me money when I ask,
What shall I do with this life you gave me
That cannot be junked like a bicycle when it wears out?

Is it utterly ridiculous for a man thirty-five years old and graying
To sit in his father's lap and ask for a bike? Even if he needs one?
Whom shall he ask if not his father?
Daddy, darling daddy, please buy me a bicycle.

Chopin

Chopin is such a great composer
I can even write poetry while his music is on the radio
Which is unusual for me.
He makes my fingers nimble like ballerinas on the keys.
He says, Let's go to town slambang on the whole goddam
      machine.

I love you Chopin in spite of the million fingers
Of little girls with long bobbing curls
Practicing your notes during daylight hours
But mostly three to five after school.
You set the hands of the children of the world
Grubbing at the keyboard
Like Pavlova put them on their wobbly toes.

I love you Chopin in spite of Merle Oberon
Although that was a pretty good movie where sweet Paul Muni
Still had two good eyes to see you were a genius.
I liked how he made you fight for Polish nationalism
That dead duck with two heads;
But of course really he was urging you
Not to turn over the Jews to the Germans
And your fingers flew like mad to save them,
But you couldn't save them since piano playing
Never saves anyone except the player if he's cute besides
(Like Van Cliburn walking through the iron curtain).
Anyway when my mother was a girl in Poland
It had become a nation already, a nation of Jewhaters
So it couldn't have been the result of your gorgeous music
Which clearly says, Love the Jews.

Chopin, my soul,
Don't listen to those critics with their dried-up eyes;
They don't like me either, my poems embarrass them.
You are too good for them
So if they want to snub you, let them,
Let them miss out on all the fun in life
Like making love and dancing about and being Mediterranean,
Still acting silly and uncynical like sixteen,
Like promising to love forever and ever and ever and doing it.

Ode to Fidel Castro

I

O Boy God, Muse of Poets
Come sit on my shoulder while I write
Cuddle up and fill my poem with love
And even while I fly on billows of inspiration
Don't forget to tickle me now and then
For I am going to write on World Issues
Which demands laughter where we most believe.

Also, My Cute One, don't let me take a heroic pose
And act as though I know it all
Guard me from Poet's Head that dread disease
Where the words ring like gongs and meaning goes out the
        window
Remind me of the human size of truth
Whenever I spout a big, ripe absolute
(Oh why did you let the architects of our capital city
Design it for giants
So that a man just has to take a short walk and look about
For exhaustion to set in immediately)
Please, Sweet Seeker, don't discourage me from contradicting
        myself
But make everything sound like life, like people we like
And most of all give me strength not to lay aside this poem
Like so many others in the pile by my typewriter
But to write the whole thing from beginning to end
O Perfection, the way it wants to go.

II

My subject, Dear Muse, is Fidel Castro
Rebellissimo and darling of the Spanish-American lower classes
A general who adopted for his uniform
The work clothes of the buck private and the beard of the saints
A man fit for ruling a great nation
But who only has an island.

Irene, the beautiful Cuban, has his picture over her bed
Between Rudolph Valentino and the Blessed Virgin—
He stands large and flabby between the perfect body and the
      purest soul
Doves on his shoulders, on his open hands
And one dove for crown standing on his head—
He is not afraid of birdshit, his face is radiant.

Someday Hollywood will make a movie biography of his life
Starring the spreading Marlon Brando
They'll invent a great love on his way up, a blonde with a large
      crucifix
Whom he loses along with his idealism, and once at the top
A great passion, a dark whore with large breasts, to drag him
      down.
In real life his romance is with his people and his role
Otherwise his sex life is normal for his age and position.

Fidel, Fidel, Fidel . . .
I am in love with the spotlight myself
And would like the crowds to chant my name
Which has the same letters as yours but rearranged
Where is my island Where my people
What am I doing on this continent Where is my crown
Where did everyone go that used to call me king
And light up like votive candles when I smiled?
(I have given them all up for you sweet youth my muse
Be truly mine.)

Am I like Goethe who kept faith in Napoleon
Long after the rest of the world had given him up
For tyrant and betrayer of the revolution?
If Napoleon was like Tolstoy writing a novel
Organizing a vast army of plots and themes
Then Castro is like a poet writing an ode
(Alas that poets should be rulers—
Revise that line, cut that stanza, lop off that phrase)
Paredon! Paredon!

What he did was kick out the bad men and good riddance Batista
What he is doing . . . Well, what he is trying to do is . . .
(Muse, why don't you help me with this,
Are you scared of socialist experiment?)
One thing he is doing is upsetting a lot of people
Our papers are full of stories that make him out a devil
And you a fool if you like him
But they are against me too even if they don't know I exist
So let's shake Fidel
(The hand that exists shakes the hand that doesn't)
My Fidel Castro, Star of Cuba.

III

The Hotel Teresa in Harlem is a dumpy landmark in a slum
But when Fidel Castro went there to stay
And when Nikita Khrushchev went up and hugged and kissed
      him for being Mr. Wonderful
Right out in public (they get away with it those foreigners)
Then Harlem became the capital of the world
And the true home of the united nations.

That whole bunch sitting around the hotel like in bivouac roasting
      chickens
And all those Negroes looking at them bugeyed—
Nobody that great ever came up there before to stay.
Of course plenty of people that great came out of Harlem
Like Jim Baldwin, not to mention those jazz people we all love

But the Colored that came out of Harlem like roman candles
You don't catch them going back there like a Fourth of July
       parade.

Now Cuba and Russia have gone to Harlem
And found it a good place for loving—
That Harlem, full of rats chewing off babies' arms
And social workers trying to keep the whole place from
       exploding
I used to have friends up there
When I went to visit them if I passed a mirror
My whiteness would surprise me
The mind takes on darkness of skin so easily
(Of course being a Jew I'm not exactly white)
It is that easy to turn black
And then have to be in that awful boat the Negroes are in
Although it's pretty lousy being white
And having that black hatred turned on you.

What after all can a white man say but, I'm ashamed
Hey fellas I'm sorry . . .
Unless you are President and then you have your golden
       opportunity.
Perhaps the only thing to do is look upon each other
As two men look when they meet solitary in the deep woods
Come black man let us jerk off together
Like boys do to get to know each other.

Well just like others who have escaped ghettos I don't go to
       Harlem anymore
I don't like to see the trapped whom I can't set free
But when I see the big front-page photos of Castro and
       Khrushchev hugging in Harlem
A widescreen spectacle with supermen in totalscope embrace, and
       in color yet
I sit back and dig it all the way
Man it swings.

IV

BOMBS GOING OFF ALL OVER HAVANA
In Rockefeller Center the Cuban Tourist Office is closed
And across the skating rink men are putting up
The world's largest Christmas tree which will never be Christian
Even if you cut it down, make it stand on cement, decorate it
      with balls
It will still scream for the forest, like a wild animal
Like the gods who love freedom and topple to the saws of
      commerce
The gods who frighten us half to death in our dreams with their
      doings
And disappear when we need them most, awake.

By the time you see this, Fidel, you might not even exist anymore
My government is merciless and even now
The machine to destroy you is moving into action
The chances are you won't last long
Well so long pal it was nice knowing you
I can't go around with a broken heart all my life
After I got over the fall of the Spanish Republic
I guess I can get over anything
My job is just to survive.

But I wish you well Fidel Castro
And if you do succeed in making that island
The tropic paradise God meant it to be
I'll be the first to cheer and come for a free visit if invited.

So you're not perfect, poets don't look for perfect
It's your spirit we love and the glamor of your style
I hope someday the cameras of the world
Are turned on you and me in some spot like Harlem
And then you'll get a kiss that will make Khrushchev's be
      forgotten
A kiss of the poet, that will make you truly good
The way you meant to be.

A Birthday Poem for My Little Sister

Ball of cold metals, shooter of nerve rays, Moon,
Be god yet for poets and their strange loves
Call in the tides of madness that trip us on our way
And help me send a poem of love to my sweet sister
Still darling like when she was a baby
Although now woman-shaped and married.

Dear Barbara, when you had the ear operation
And your hair was cut short like a baby dike
I sat by your crib because I considered you mine
And read you stories of cluck-cluck and moo-moo:
They didn't have to make sense, just noises.

I tried to keep you from masturbating
According to instructions in Parents' Magazine
Which recommended the diversion method rather than threats or
    punishment.
It was no use, your hand preferred your little cunt to toys I
    offered
Like the ape in the zoo who was jerking off
And all the kids asked their mothers, "What's he doing, ma?"
So the keeper tried to divert him from his hard-on with an ice-
    cream cone
But he shifted the cone to the other hand and licked it while he
    went right on.

And then during the war we were both in uniform
You in the Brownies and I in the Air Force:
When I came home that time with silver wings on
You threw yourself into my arms like a furry bundle;
That was your contribution to the war effort, a hug for a soldier
Not bombing the Germans as you were convinced the Brownies
    were going to do.

When you were twelve I saw your intellectual possibilities
And took you to a difficult play
Where you fell in love with the big faggot actor.
Then I tried modern poetry on you, The Love Song of J. Alfred
      Prufrock;
You listened very seriously and remembered the refrain like a
      jump-rope poem:
It was odd to hear a little girl reciting those lines.

And suddenly you grew up and went out with boys . . . strangers
And you spoke with them in a language like a code
I mean you became a woman, so I'll never have you again:
There must be some taboo against brothers.
Of course now I have someone of my own who reaches to me
      with sweet arms
But the heart is a tree of many seasons
And old loves grow forever deep inside.

The moon rules old loves in their branching
And today the great white magic ball in the sky
Has wound up my heart like on a line of wool
Today on your birthday I remember
How I ran up and down the block knocking on all the doors
To tell the neighbors you were born
(Bored looks, after all you were the sixth child):
I was really announcing that you were born for me and would be
      mine.

But you grew up and went away and got married
As little girls grow up into women
Leaving us gasping and desperate and hurt.
And we recover and forget, or half-forget
Until sitting down to write a birthday poem we remember
      everything—
A little girl on her potty hunched seriously to the business
Or holding all of you at once in my arms, colt, calf, and pussy-cat:
All I mean is, I miss you my little sister.

Mark Twain and Sholem Aleichem

Mark Twain and Sholem Aleichem went one day to Coney
    Island—
Mark wearing a prison-striped bathing costume and straw hat,
Sholem in greenish-black suit, starched collar, beard,
Steelrimmed schoolmaster glasses, the whole works,
And an umbrella that he flourished like an actor
Using it sometimes to hurry along the cows
As he described scenes of childhood in the village in Poland,
Or to spear a Jew on a sword like a cossack.

Sitting together on the sand among food wrappers and lost coins,
They went through that famous dialogue
Like the vaudeville routine, After-you-Gaston:
"They tell me you are called the Yiddish Mark Twain."
"Nu? The way I heard it you are the American Sholem
    Aleichem."
And in this way passed a pleasant day admiring each other,
The voice of the old world and the voice of the new.

"Shall we risk the parachute jump, Sholem?"
"Well, Markele, am I properly dressed for it?
Better we should go in the water a little maybe?"
So Sholem Aleichem took off shoes and socks (with holes—a
    shame),
Rolled up stiff-serge pants showing his varicose veins;
And Mark Twain, his bathing suit moth-eaten and gaping
In important places, lit up a big cigar,
And put on a pair of waterwings like an angel.

The two great writers went down where the poor
Were playing at the water's edge
Like a sewer full of garbage, warm as piss.
Around them shapeless mothers and brutal fathers

Were giving yellow, brown, white, and black children
Lessons in life that the ignorant are specially qualified to give:
Slaps and scoldings, mixed with food and kisses.

Mark Twain, impetuous goy, dived right in,
And who could resist splashing a little the good-natured Jew?
Pretty soon they were both floundering in the sea
The serge suit ruined that a loving daughter darned and pressed,
The straw hat floating off on the proletarian waters.

They had both spent their lives trying to make the world a better
    place
And both had gently faced their failure.
If humor and love had failed, what next?
They were both drowning and enjoying it now,
Two old men of the two worlds, the old and the new,
Splashing about in the sea like crazy monks.

Tulips and Addresses

The Museum of Modern Art on West Fifty-third Street
Is interested only in the flower not the bulb:
After the Dutch tulips finished blooming in the garden last year
They pulled them up and threw them away—that place has no
    heart.
Some fortunately were rescued and came into my possession.

I kept them all winter in a paper bag from the A & P
At first where I was living then on the Westside
Until the next-door tribe of Murphies drove me out with rock and
    roll,
Then at Thompson Street in the Village where overhead
A girl and her lover tromped around all night on each other.

And that wasn't the end of it: I shlepped those bulbs around
For two months from place to place looking for a home,
All that winter, moving . . . Oy—although this was nothing new
    for me
Coming as I do from a wandering race,
And life with its ten plagues making me even more Jewish.

Now I am living on Abingdon Square, not the Ritz exactly, but a
    place
And I have planted the tulips in my window box:
Please God make them come up, so that everyone who passes by
Will know I'm there, at least long enough to catch my breath,
When they see the bright red beautiful flowers in my window.

The Sleeper

When I was the sissy of the block who nobody wanted on their
team
Sonny Hugg persisted in believing that my small size was an asset
Not the liability and curse I felt it was
And he saw a use for my swift feet with which I ran away from
fights.

He kept putting me into complicated football plays
Which would have been spectacular if they worked:
For instance, me getting clear in front and him shooting the ball
over—
Or the sensation of the block, the Sleeper Play
In which I would lie down on the sidelines near the goal
As though resting and out of action, until the scrimmage began
And I would step onto the field, receive the long throw
And to the astonishment of all the tough guys in the world
Step over the goal line for a touchdown.

That was the theory anyway. In practice
I had the fatal flaw of not being able to catch
And usually had my fingers bent back and the breath knocked out
of me
So the plays always failed, but Sonny kept on trying
Until he grew up out of my world into the glamorous
Varsity crowd, the popular kids of Lynbrook High.

But I will always have this to thank him for:
That when I look back on childhood
(That four psychiatrists haven't been able to help me bear the
thought of)
There is not much to be glad for
Besides his foolish and delicious faith
That, with all my oddities, there was a place in the world for me
If only he could find the special role.

At the Coney Island Aquarium:

An Ode for Ookie,
the Older Walrus Child

or

The Sibling Rival

Do not worry, sweet little walrus, about the superior cuteness
Of those two new babies they brought to share your pool.

You keep pushing the twins out of the way
More concerned about keeping them from getting attention
Than having your own scrub-brush nose whiskers rubbed
So that no one gets the chance to give you
The endless hugs and kisses you deserve.

It is impossible of course to be more popular than twins
So finally you sink to the bottom and play dead
Hoping our hearts break—mine does anyway
And the Keeper watches anxiously, so you see it works.
But how long can you sit at the bottom of the water
When lungs cry for air and the heart for love?

No, Ookie, don't seek indiscriminate love from the many
As those two simple-minded children do
Who have not yet met with heartbreak (although they will),
But leap the railing right into my arms
And squirm there fishily always, Ookie, mine alone.

The Garden

The plants on the window ledges are all growing well
Except the avocado which is dying

The grapefruit seeds from breakfast came up
And the watermelon are sprouting all over the window box

The mango practically exploded it looked so pregnant
Cherry, peach, apple and plum trees flourish

The potato eyes threw up weird white shoots
And the birdseed grew a good crop of ragweed

We have formed a colony in a strange land
Planting our seeds and making ourselves at home

The laws are our own to make except those of growth
Which are God's and we obey His alone

I look around this place, everything in order
The implements of living stacked

Fishes in the stream blowing bubbles like kisses
Wild cats to drag yowling from the woods

Trees to hug and roots to dig
A young horse to play around with

It is a beautiful place to have the run of
When a sweet creature of your own brings all of it to you.